better together*

*This book is best read together, grownup and kid.

 akidsco.com

a kids book about

a kids book about SLEEP

by Katie Pitts
in partnership with Sleep Wise Consulting

a kids book about

Text and design copyright © 2023
by A Kids Book About, Inc.

Copyright is good! It ensures that work like this can exist, and more work in the future can be created.

All rights reserved. No part of this publication may be reproduced, distributed, or transmitted in any form or by any means, including photocopying, recording, other electronic or mechanical methods, without the prior written permission of the publisher, except in the case of brief quotations embodied in critical reviews and certain other noncommercial uses permitted by copyright law. For permission requests, write to the publisher.

A Kids Book About, Kids Are Ready, and the colophon 'a' are trademarks of A Kids Book About, Inc.

Printed in the United States of America.

A Kids Book About books are available online: *akidsco.com*

To share your stories, ask questions, or inquire about bulk purchases (schools, libraries, and nonprofits), please use the following email address: *hello@akidsco.com*

Print ISBN: 978-1-958825-56-3
Ebook ISBN: 978-1-958825-55-6

Designed by Jelani Memory
Edited by Emma Wolf

The author would like to thank Chris Baptiste. From the first to final draft, she was a magical wordsmith, and this book truly wouldn't be what it is today without her.

I dedicate this book to my family of boys, for without them, I wouldn't know how desperately sought after and deeply needed a full night of rest really is.

I also dedicate this book to my amazing team. Thank you for not only supporting my big ideas, but sharing your knowledge of sleep with so many.

Intro

I can pretty much guarantee that, at one time or another throughout your life—and especially on your parenting journey—sleep will be a popular topic of discussion.

Every part of your mental, emotional, and physical performance is impacted by the quality of your sleep. And the same is true for your kid. We all know our kids need sleep, but helping them get it is another story.

Giving our kids information about why sleep is so important, acknowledging why it can be hard, and sharing some strategies to feel good at bedtime can empower our kids to take control of their sleep.

I hope this book provides a moment of connection and calm before a night of restful sleep!

Oh, good! You're awake.

I want to tell you about sleep
and why it's so important.

Why everyone needs it.

In fact, all living, breathing things
need sleep (even your pet turtle or hamster).

SO, WHAT IS SLEEP?

Sleep is when you close your eyes for

a long period of time, usually at night.

It might feel short to you. It might feel reeeeeee

eeeeeeeeeeeeeeeeeeeeeeeeeeeeeeeeeeeeeeeeally long.

And mostly, you might think sleep is just something your grownups make you do.

But getting good, healthy sleep is a really big deal!

When we fall asleep,
our brain and body are doing...

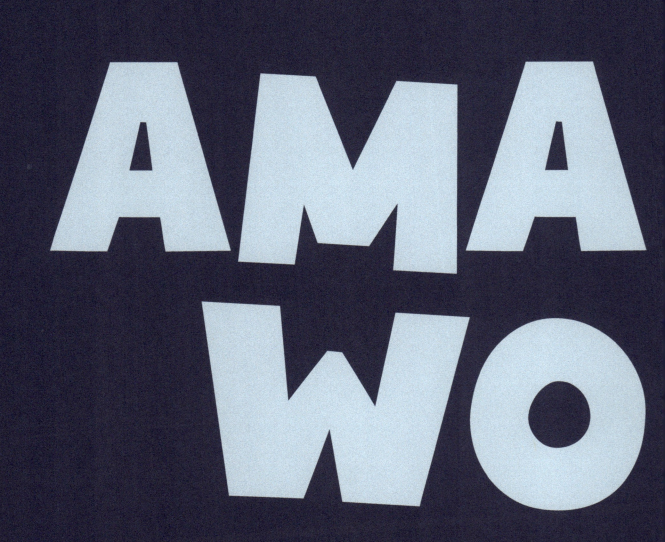

ZING RK.

When you get good sleep,
it makes you feel great!

SLEEP HELPS US

RUN, JUMP, PLAY, LEARN, GROW, HEAL, THINK, STAY HEALTHY, FEEL GOOD, PROBLEM-SOLVE, BE CREATIVE, REGULATE OUR EMOTIONS, LIVE A LONG LIFE, STORE MEMORIES, FEEL CALMER, STAY COORDINATED,

SOLVE PUZZLES, DRIVE A CAR, PUT OUR SHOES ON, REMEMBER TO WEAR UNDERWEAR, ACE THAT TEST, SWIM, RIDE BIKES, JUMP ON THE COUCH, DANCE, SCOOP ICE CREAM, KEEP OUR BRAIN HEALTHY (AND MORE!).

Sleep allows us to fully recharge for the next day, like a battery powering up.

There is a certain amount of sleep that everyone needs to be fully recharged, and it's different for everyone.

Kids, like you, need between
9 and 11 hours of sleep each night.
And that may seem like a long time!

Grownups don't need as much.
They typically get **8 or 9 hours of sleep.***

*Your grownup may try to tell you they can get by with
less than that. Make sure they know that isn't true!

You might be wondering...

WHY DO KIDS NEED SO MUCH SLEEP?

Well, kids are growing and changing at a pretty fast rate. Your body and brain need those extra hours at night to renew and recharge.

Also, think about all the activities you do every day. Do you read, write, or color? Do you play games at recess? Do you go to the park?

All of these things take energy, and that energy comes from sleeping well!

So, a good bedtime for kids is usually between 7:30 and 8:30 p.m. And for grownups, going to bed around 10 p.m. makes the most sense.

I know it might seem really unfair if you're the first person to go to bed every night.

But really, sleep is an amazing, wonderful thing.

I also know there are reasons why sleep doesn't seem amazing to you (yet).

Reasons like…

NIGHTMARES. MISSING YOUR LONELY. NIGHTTIME FEELS LIKE YOU'D RATHER WATCH TV. **YOU'D** WITH YOUR FRIENDS. **YOU FEEL LIKE** YOU'RE NOT EVEN TIRED! (YOU TELLING YOU WHAT TO DO.) **YOUR** YOUR DRESS-UP CLOTHES ARE PAJAMAS. **YOU'RE TOO HUNGRY TO SLEEP.** EVEN DOING THE DISHES WITH THEIR CHORES SOUNDS

GROWNUP AT NIGHT. FEELING FOREVER. IT'S DARK OUTSIDE. RATHER READ. YOU'D RATHER PLAY YOU'RE NOT GOOD AT SLEEPING. *ARE* TIRED OF YOUR GROWNUPS TOYS ARE SO MUCH MORE FUN. WAY COOLER THAN YOUR SLEEP. YOU'RE TOO THIRSTY TO OR HELPING YOUR GROWNUPS BETTER THAN GOING TO SLEEP!

Any of these reasons
make sense for why
you wouldn't want to sleep.

The truth is, **SLEEP IS ONE OF THE BEST THINGS YOU CAN DO TO STAY HEALTHY.**

Remember those batteries we were talking about earlier?

You might think you feel **OK** with a 25% or 50% charge, but inside, your brain isn't operating at its best.

It might show up in different ways throughout your day: forgetting an answer on a test you studied hard for, tripping and falling during a soccer game, arguing with a friend, or just not feeling like yourself.

Does any of that sound familiar to you?

You won't get perfect sleep every night.
That's part of being human!

BUT REMEMBER, THERE'S A NEW CHANCE FOR GOOD SLEEP EACH NIGHT.

So, how can you make falling asleep and staying asleep feel easier?

I have some ideas for you to try!

But first, I want to let you in on a little secret.

The best way to sleep well is...

TO NOT THINK ABOUT SLEEP AT ALL.

DID I JUST JUST BLOW YOUR MIND?

I promise it's true!

So, here are 3 things to think about instead.

1.

Focus on taking some

DEEP BREATHS

at bedtime, like you're blowing BIG bubbles carefully.

Place your hands on your belly so you can feel it get bigger as you take a deep breath. Then, let it out really **slooooowly.**

This kind of breathing calms you and tells your body it's time to relax.

2.

Try taking an
IMAGINATION VACATION.

This can be a really great tool if you get nightmares.

Close your eyes and think about the place you feel the happiest in the world.

WHO IS THERE WITH YOU?

WHAT ARE YOU DOING THERE?

WHAT'S THE WEATHER LIKE?

WHAT DOES IT SMELL LIKE?

HOW DOES BEING THERE MAKE YOU FEEL?

Let this place be the last thing you think about before you fall asleep.

3.

And one more thing you can try is **USING A MANTRA,** which is an encouraging phrase or sentence that helps you feel calm.

Some examples are:

I AM LOVED.
I AM SAFE.
I AM COZY.

Pick one, combine them,
or create your own!

Try writing your mantra and keeping it by your bed.

That way, if you wake up or have trouble sleeping, those words are right there and will help you fall back asleep.

The great news is that *you* have the POWER over your sleep.

You know why sleep is so important.

And now you have some
tools to help you sleep well.

Sleep matters for everyone.

And for you, the kid,
it's your time to grow,
recharge your batteries,
and wake up to be...

THE
BEST
YOU
THAT
YOU
CAN BE.

Outro

Sleep can often elicit some big feelings from our kids, and as grownups, we have our own experiences that shape how we feel about sleep, too. The good news is that you and your kid are now armed with information and tools to help you both feel good about sleep.

Here are 3 more suggestions to help you continue your kid's healthy sleep journey:

1. Set a predictable bedtime routine to help prepare for sleep every evening.

2. Limit screen time an hour or more before bed to allow melatonin to increase naturally.

3. Navigate nightmares with empathy, without letting it derail sleep. (The frequency of nightmares often decreases when a kid is well-rested.)

The goal is for bedtime to be a peaceful part of the day, followed by a full night of sleep. Oh, and in case we didn't mention it, these strategies will work for you too!

About The Author

Katie (she/her) wrote this book for kids of all ages who might not know yet just how good sleep can feel. For Katie, sleep always came easily, and it wasn't until her 2 kids came along that she realized the same wasn't true for them.

Sometimes sleep can feel hard, but it doesn't have to be that way night after night.

Through her work at Sleep Wise Consulting and writing this book, Katie is on a mission to educate and empower kids to think about sleep differently—not as something to neglect, but as something to cherish. And perhaps, this book will make a great addition to your bedtime routine!

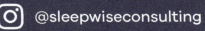 @sleepwiseconsulting   @sleepwiseconsulting

 SleepWiseConsulting.com

 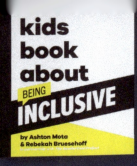   
 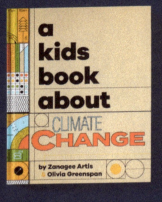  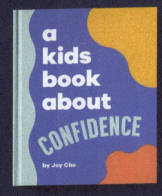 
 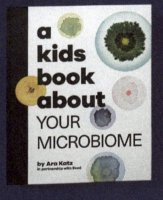 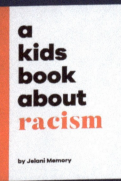 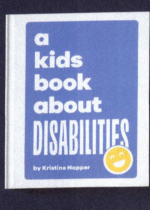 
  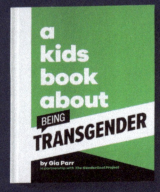 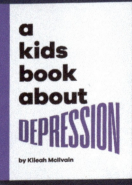 

Discover more at akidsco.com

Printed in the USA
CPSIA information can be obtained
at www.ICGtesting.com
LVHW071939290923
759708LV00012B/206